THE FLY IN AUTUMN

Books by David Zieroth

The Village of Sliding Time (2006)
The Education of Mr. Whippoorwill: A Country Boyhood (2002)
Crows Do Not Have Retirement (2001)
How I Joined Humanity At Last (1998)
The Weight of My Raggedy Skin (1991)
When the Stones Fly Up (1985)
Mid-River (1981)
Clearing: Poems from a Journey (1973)

THE FLY IN AUTUMN

poems

David Zieroth

HARBOUR PUBLISHING

1 2 3 4 5 — 13 12 11 10 09

Harbour Publishing Co. Ltd.
P.O. Box 219, Madeira Park, BC, V0N 2H0
www.harbourpublishing.com

Cover illustration by Marjalena Zieroth.
Printed and bound in Canada.
Printed on 100% PCW stock.

Harbour Publishing acknowledges financial support from the Government of Canada through the Book Publishing Industry Development Program and the Canada Council for the Arts, and from the Province of British Columbia through the BC Arts Council and the Book Publishing Tax Credit.

Library and Archives Canada Cataloguing in Publication

Zieroth, David
The fly in autumn / David Zieroth.

Poems.
ISBN 978-1-55017-468-7

I. Title.

PS8599.I47F49 2009 C811'.54 C2009-900886-6

"All the efforts of the human mind cannot exhaust the essence of a single fly."

—St. Thomas Aquinas

"All liminalities belong entirely to the mind, and we are perverse if we expect the objective world to keep to our categories."

—James Hamilton-Paterson, *Seven-Tenths: The Sea and Its Thresholds*

CONTENTS

ACKNOWLEDGEMENTS

Grateful thanks to the editors of the following publications where some of these poems first appeared (sometimes in earlier versions):

BC Studies, Event, Facets, The Fiddlehead, Grain, The Malahat Review, The Modern Review, Nthposition, poetry strand 2008, The Seattle Review, Singing Crow, The Vancouver Review, The Windsor Review, Palominos and other poems (Gaspereau, 2000), *Rocksalt* (Mother Tongue Publishing, 2008).

"Hollow" has been produced as a broadsheet with artwork by Daniel Koppersmith.

I am also thankful for the support of the friends and writers who helped with the writing and the writing-time of these poems, especially Robert Adams, gillian harding-russell, Richard Lemm, Lorna McCallum, Meg Stainsby, Richard Therrien and Russell Thornton. And Silas White for his editorial guidance.

1.

Man in the Ice Fog

MAN IN THE ICE FOG

The man in the ice fog tugs his hat down
and tries to believe that somewhere sun
    shines hard on beaches, hot dog buns,
    scrambling children, waves, a seaside town
laughing at its own leisure, boys watching legs,
and wives and mothers turning a little to beg

from their men something more, then giving
up and taking sand in their hands: enough
    for now. The man in the fog scuffs
    his shoe against cold unforgiving
stones; their grey blank layers don't change,
he knows, for even in day-bright they're strange

unremarkable chunks—like him today,
earthbound, unable to walk beyond this mist
    and past his own absurdist
    ache: that all life (plus his) has slid away
and pulses in some upper sunny
realm, light like pure honey.

AT NIGHT I TAKE OFF MY GLASSES

At night I take off my glasses
to look at dreams more clearly
my last act before sleep
to remove the light of reason
I lie down into the hollering
blood and fluids that spill
scalding, and crying aloud
some word or name I lose
as close to me as even I can get

At night I stop what I have seen
so plainly all day: how I smiled
when I should have turned away
caught by the shake of a hand
the spittle on the lips
and what leaps from the gleam of an eye
and cannot be said in words
leaps still, as a bird strikes up
flushed from the cover of its bush

In morning's first sheen I reach over
and place onto my face, apply to myself
what is necessary to see my way through
what I have done by becoming me
creator and co-creator
but it is not the maze of my making
that catches me up so much
rather I stumble when a dream returns
suddenly in my way

some hot mess that twists
rising up like smoke or steam to show
the crack of the world is finally here
so I must look, bent forward, tipping
with the weight of wishfulness
and begin the slide
headlong, into the opening earth
my eyes shocked open by descent

and nothing to grasp
rust and cold cannot be held
light comes up from a far figure
where fog surrounds him, and I
can see will soon be me
spread out immeasurably thin
as mist is thin, then gone

PALOMINOS

Nineteen palominos
fling themselves
across the field till the first
stumbles, goes down
fetlock flailing

Those behind
trip, twist white manes
around their necks
start to roll under
where eyes see dirt

Yet they drive toward me
falling and sinking hooves
into ribs
and powerful haunches
that cannot be stopped

I see no masters
the chariot each pulls
empty, wheels tipped
then dragged
over stones

Blood in the dust
long bones crack
then break, so I begin to count
the numbers not rising but writhing
I must fire upon

And then they are saved
perhaps by blondness
One reaches me, nuzzles
my hand, sweating, snorting
but not afraid

and the others, even those
who plunged and sank
push through a curtain
a veil of my wishing
all their carts upright

HOW BRAVE

> . . . make a complete exit from life, not
> in anger, but simply, freely, with integrity,
> making this leaving of it at least one
> achievement in your life.
>
> —Marcus Aurelius, *Meditations*

How brave of a worldly one dying
on his white antiseptic bed to say
there is no god and I have become death
his last breath a final simple heaving
not extending upwards into arms
of waiting deities, his forehead damp
not with excitement or exaltation
but effort of animal exertion that must
be borne, yes, and thus he suffers
the magnitude of the task, of leaving
corporeal substance, the scrabbling hand
and even what's called consciousness
the flame that asks always why *is*
feels both unborn and deathless

How bravely those who cannot believe
meet the moment when an afterlife
begins for others, not them, and how
they stay stoic, having learned ways
not to hope or despair—denying either—
but to penetrate the mystery of the day
in mornings when they live clear headed
—in afternoons they sag, work-logged—

in evenings when they stop to weigh
the stars, imagining not so much
themselves arriving as dust from such
a distance, nor being small beyond
meaning itself—just breathing hearts
beating numbers, recognizing time

How brave to die when we can't behold
our parents arriving to greet our souls
embarking apparently from pale beds where
we fight for the dignity of our aloneness
though clustered around by attendant
machines and our bewildered children
How we have raged for our right not to be
herded by churchy cherubs, not to further
cosmic harmonics in our progression from
matter toward what can hardly be said
To enter rot and raise no arm and shout!
To prepare our gratitude and give back
without benefit of flood or inferno, wordlessly
what we borrowed in our mothers' wombs

ANOTHER NOUN GONE

That thing
kept in kitchens
sometimes hanging

near stoves, always with holes
often with feet, in the past
made with metal

now from plastic
(mine is red) used for draining
catching what we eat

hot and steaming, usually white
dumped and tossed
lifted up and strung down

open mouths still talking
as they chew, wine
talking too, young children near

wrecking the lilac bush
with their love of playing
while we up here, at ease

in our verandah-knowing, know
how long purple fragrance takes
to bloom! *Years* before we *said* "lilac"

more years after, at open kitchen windows
a sudden stilling, scent of mother
pinch of dad—ball, kiss, hat—

can't say all the words yet—then
flying forward to this, this
speechless-sometimes phase

more place than phase
in its rock-squat stillness, un-breathing
thing to break through

OLD WOMEN

Since light first woke and sent them loping
dogs bite through plastic, finding discards
worth wolfing down
along lanes where blue boxes
have bloomed again

Without speaking, someone in charge
has sent old women out to back streets
to return concrete to itself
They cannot re-enter their homes
without first dipping fingers in filth
produced daily by children still sleeping
and by fathers and mothers
preparing their faces in rooms at the back
The grandmothers take this time to recall
dead husbands, less substance today
than chicken bones and greasy kitchen papers
dogs have scattered

When old ones go out never to return
then weeping begins
because too late someone has a question
no one can answer
while city workers (too sleepy to see
silent shrivelled faces unremarkable
in bottoms of boxes, near roaring machines)
sort yogurt containers and label-less
cans and newspapers full of alarm

HOLLOW

Suddenly I am hollowed out, at the lip
of weeping, panic in my throat, because
  the season changes, and into the pause
  between the shifting moments slips
a blankness unprepared for, and someone's
leaving, and all my plans come undone.

Nor does it help that the dark
falls early, clouds blocking light
  so even a pleasant walk cannot ignite
  inside me the necessary spark
of hopefulness that gives a shape to each hour,
that fights off what comes to devour

the little I've now become: alone
to make the day, routine not yet kicked in.
  I kick sidewalk trash while within
  whirls my own lean cyclone
sucking from me what once I was: one whose joy
at living and arriving was not so easy to destroy.

I'D RATHER HAVE RELATIVES

I'd rather have relatives than mice
in my house, preferring nibblers I can catch
    in my arms to those that hatch
    out of holes and never cease.
I'll choose large late night cheese-eaters
over little skittering sleep-cheaters,

noise in a wall when all else is quiet,
except for our snoring dear old aunt
    whose unconscious snorting taunts
    admittedly, as we listen to the riot
in her throat, rattling from the next bedroom,
her thrashing up for air, it seems a poolroom

of mucus balls adjusting in her lungs
—and yet we know exactly where she is
    and what will happen next, no incubus
    comes for her with a long, hot tongue,
whereas in the kitchen leap tiny
forms of filth incarnate, their tails shiny.

THESE POEMS HAVE ATTITUDE

> . . . in any case, it was a change, and
> in the climate of age and decline this
> can at times be a not inconsiderable
> inducement.
>
> —Hermann Hesse,
> *Autobiographical Writings*

We are the people at the party wearing
the wrong clothes, the bolo tie,
    the large cuffs, though our flies
    remained zipped; we are not declaring
anything more than this: *we be here.*
Yet loose-lip hipsters hate how near

we stand to one another, in our tight rows,
how easily we break into marching songs,
    not afraid to show we belong
    to something more than prose-
like uncontrolled jitterbugging moves
any fool can find once he removes

the cufflinks, bone buttons and Windsor knots.
So let them "dance," we smirk among ourselves,
    knowing their so-called grooves
    are thin, unlike the grassroots
we spring from, where being free means
living the logos, not lobbing arrhythmic smithereens.

SAY "BAGHDAD" . . .

and I turn away
say "car bomb"
and I blank
say

I'm in denial
that I have lost

electrons on my care molecule
and now my capacity to mind

wobbles like a ship, cluttered
over-cluttered, weak as paper
older, from the port of Cain

and, anyway, waiting for a death star
to find us

*

when I left teaching, I said
"I am no longer responsible

for the ignorance of the world"

from such an aggrieved statement
I knew I'd retreat, someday
I wanted to

then another bomb blew

so let the young accuse me
and children of the killed curse me
because it remains true:
I failed to maintain continuous hope

we stockpile bodies
for the day sufficient numbers
answer the question
we have all stopped asking

when air above a bomb-hole
thickens with pages
only fingers torn and blood-drained
can turn

HOW WISE

How wise to give away your books!
To keep yourself free from boxes
    when you move, paradoxes
    in every one: those words look
light and lovely on the page but turn out
leaden when you have to mess about

schlepping old classics up new stairs.
Better to hand them off one by one,
    novels to your sister, John Donne
    to anyone who still says prayers.
Keep back a few, the special heroes
of your heart who soar past the common Joes

like yourself—like me—and make a life
we couldn't make. One box of words will do,
    to fill your need for guidance into
    the new home, along with knives,
pillows, pants and postures, lamp and bed.
Sad tales of the old place stay behind (to live unsaid).

THE TRAGEDY OF HUMAN LONELINESS

for Duncan

A friend sends these words, and I read them
and imagine they are simultaneously heard
    by all persons on the planet, each stirred
    to thought and feeling by this gem
of phrasing reaching beyond mere information
to resonate with everyone.

My screen is blue today, pale, so black
words stand out, stating how solitary
    faces begin leaking, bleary
    from the force of inner flack
while others present solitude as their crown:
deep eyes, calm, nice folks to be around

but sometimes even these who
have landed, truly, at ease
    in their bodies and minds, pleased
    with both, ready to joke, even these true
humans among friends, husbands and wives
cannot always touch beyond themselves.

NOT FOREST OR WOODS BUT BUSH

Not forest with green-black belt
overflowing on and off continents
not woods with morning-melancholy
poets and winsome girls walking
in and out of dapple and alive to
evening dove's coo of farewell

but bush: tangled under-leaves meeting
low branches pointing lower yet
no booty squirreled below
no sublime unending air of mystery
just grey invitation to go elsewhere
anywhere more easily breached

Sometimes birds, if grouse are really birds
not emergency food for rabid dogs
sometimes a skunk waddles out
from edge at evening, certain he'll find
his share in Broody Hen's nest
To suckle down her fertile eggs!

Bent in their threads to the sun
branchlets follow light each day
but end in angles even bats avoid
twig-mesh for moon, holding it
while moon washes bush and makes
shapes no night-walker can abide

air and tree and bough interchanging
as being of one becomes being
of other, pale glow on faces
beneath blurring criss-cross overgrowth
only one beam penetrates
When gathered up, this ray fills

less than a cat's paw imprint
on soggy moss and dropped brush
always bouncing back—whatever walks here
leaves no trace, perfect terrain for children
murderers predators spies lost starlings
regrouping before black and yellow flight

THE FLAT

Why can no one hear me anymore?
When I start to tell my story
—flat tire on the morning road to work
jack missing and my hike back
to the 7-11 phone—the man I'm speaking to
starts talking before I'm finished
because he wants to
(a) tell me how he had a flat once
and it was raining then and so
much worse than my little situation, or
(b) explain that flat was not just a flat
but the end of the life I was living up till then
and which everyone knew was a sham
and surely now I was free to be free, or
(c) blame me for ineptness
in not having a spare jack
tucked up under the passenger's seat
where occasionally someone might feel
its hardness and wonder, call out, or
(d) slyly suggest I might find a woman
willing to buttress and buoy me
so I need not drive to work at all
could stay home, learn Szechuan cooking, or
(e) give me a pamphlet calling for volunteers
to sweat in foreign countries where real
unfortunates live, where I might meet them
face to face and grow in understanding
beyond my present half-knowledge, or
(f) pat my shoulder, stroke my arm

point out my shoes are dusty
from roadside grime
where dry grasses swept back by air
forced upon them by five-ton trucks
speak to crinkly trash they hold
industrial beauty about to be broken down
into hushed new pieces of dirt

SO THE SNOW

So the snow comes down, falling through
a cone of streetlight's yellow cast.
    At work, on our warm side of glass,
    I watch how easily my view
can change to white, cold slipping
past fool efforts of weather stripping.

Years ago I would have frolicked
in the stuff, turned my hands red
    aiming snowballs at heads
    that ducked: a winter bucolic.
Now I pray to cloudy gods to stop
this mess: think of the roads, the icy slop

I trudge through, slowly stepping home,
my feet freezing, fretting that some car will spin
    out of control, kill me, next of kin
    not yet aware I've eaten chrome,
head crunched open on crimson ice,
steaming words spilling without a voice.

AM I DREAMING?

"Am I dreaming? Has the time come?"
He'd hoped to stay a year or two
    away from today's overdue
    moment when he suddenly becomes
someone who steps out on a morning and then
halts, turns back, hears not the house wren

but his old blood pumping, calling him
to bear the weight of memory, all the *done*
    deeds impossible now to shun,
    their accumulation (however slight) so grim
he cannot pass; gargoyles at his door,
hideously grey, would be easier to ignore

than the thoughts that slow him down.
He examines one, and then it's noon,
    looks at another—and now the moon
    brings its silver light to drown
the last hope he has: that this day would
come later and by then be better understood.

JUST TWO STREETS DOWN

Just two streets down, a ship booms
from its loudest iron horn
    a sound of deepest mourning
    (a slow wet sound in a low dark tomb)
someone might hear were he asleep
and dreaming of lovers who made him weep.

A corroded creature, commerce
hauls into harbour below his street
    the edict that everyone greet
    cheerily this load forged from forces
in far bolder lands, some mythic,
some poor, one or two monolithic

at providing auto parts, fish sauce
and shoddy shirts; and yet
    as he glides further into foreign debt
    he's not thinking of pocket loss
but of his boyhood hope: to be brave,
to ship out, to learn to sleep on waves.

2.

Netted Gems

NETTED GEMS

Who was that woman at the downward tunnel
and why had I stopped at its entrance
to steal a potato
from her basket
bosom full with Netted Gems

And those other women crossing the stream
how did they know to place the foot
just so on rocks
hidden by the glare of glass light
three of seven
gripping babies on their hips
as they bent under boughs
and moved down the trail
hidden once, twice by spear grass
flaming up from well-washed stones

Those fat babies
floating on past trunks and shrubs
their wet smiles turning back
—and soon plumped down
in duff and sun
to sleep
where one gazes up, round
mouth full and warm
till someone says
wake up, little piggy man
your time is now
and a finger touches my head

DICK AND FAMOUS JANE

It is a truth universally acknowledged
that young guys in hot cars
like to be noticed:
their muscles, their tans
their arms pressed against
steering wheels and forcing them
back into leather seats, their rings
their short stiff thick hair
sunglasses with straight arms
never bending behind the ear

What is less well known
a secret, really, is who they want
beside them: a blonde
someone called Jane, a literary
type, famous for words, but now
silenced by wind rushing
into the convertible, the bass
in his music so loud she can feel it
vibrating her seat

causing sentences to be formed
complete whole thoughts
ready to be written down
for him, about him
how his love for himself
is turning toward her
she of windy hair and Scandinavian bones
hands so thin and weightless

except upon him, words her finger
can write upon skin
up and down his spine

that later make him want
to drive, fast, car leaping
away from touch
into open air, road silent
except for grooves
suctioning pavement

NIGHT WALK

Walking up K Road in the dark
sidewalk wet and running
cars hurrying down slant
toward, I presume, happiness

I would be a quick leap
into metal and light
thump and rolling under
jeans torn, muscles jumping

Strong men lift me
into a sad face
who scissors up
my pant-leg, white cotton
pads coming away red: flags
from the authority of the body
telling me I must stay

Death alone
could not supply
the intimacy needed
to cherish flesh
Some softer fall was called for:
blood on bone
bone broken
eyes jammed shut
the slow returning to self

planted in a sterile bed
to learn how a man can walk
in the unimaginable days
holding onto rails
smiling at cheerfulness

FUSS POEM

I want to be fucking someone
who wants to be fucking me:
    arms, throats, lips along the knees,
    while hard and soft the spirit runs
between our tips and out beyond
our little bed, until we correspond

with sweetness all about us
that every day we miss when we fail
    to love enough—and so we rail
    at the world, or at least I fuss
if my lot isn't filled with flesh and froth,
that moment we drop clothes

off our sweating bodies, and eye to eye
manifest our dreams of lust
    when once again—*yes!*—we thrust
    ourselves upon ourselves, cry
out and come dumbstruck
in the fury gained by those who fuck.

THE LOVER SAYS *WHATEVER*

Let's not be precise one more moment.
Who cares if *farther* is not *further*?
    Let our sentences slur
    and slip, sloppy in their descent
until what I have to say to you
becomes some meady brew

of grunts and clicks, uh, uh, *ah*
and you read my face and smile,
    convinced that all the while
    I'm confessing undying yeah
yeah booms away, sweet, sweet.
I could just as well discuss the defeat

of the plain speech movement
when you've got that look, clothes
    tossed aside until each of us knows
    words are pure torment
and might as well be flung and gone,
wherever, say, Azerbaijan.

ALL OF LIFE WE PRACTISE DYING . . .

as happens in a young man's
untenderness toward his girl
and himself turned newly cold
by entry into work and money—
all of life we practise change

trying on the final unfleshing
yet only once allowed to show
how well we've trained: *once only*
no trial run, lead-up or heats
and no chance of winning

in the switch from *if* to *when*—
days before their 50th gathering
the husband's heart falls
dead before him, his wife hours later
attacked by her brain

lives on, surgeons masterful
at allowing her lastborn to return
from camping with wife and sons
to reflect first on his late father
then his mother's almost-following

to think, in *his* shift, "we kiss
the loved one for the last time
and don't know it," each day
closer to a blood-bursting
remembering daily he will die

slowly he unearths that asking why
is a way to prayer, to soften and
enter the quietus after rage
and sometimes at the start of sleep
his sons' faces rise in his mind

HOW TO WALK IN THE DARK WITH FLOWERS

Open your eyes to the light
in the armful of lilies you are holding

Move forward and be guided
by the sheen of their white curves
quavering stamens of dizzy gold
shimmering back at you as you

take the first step
A torch of flower-light
does not allow itself
to feel
cut from the earth
Just think: to be beautiful
and dying at the same, last time

Lay the lilies down on the body
Leave them, and say goodbye

Now, groping along
on hands and knees
the help you need
you generate yourself
as you wait for lucidity
to descend
with its burden
of resolve

which you'll readily embrace, arms eager
glad to push upright again
dark clay at a good distance
wind from the sky heaping around you
living aromas
from beings of light someone planted
many years ago

WATER-LIGHT

I am beginning to watch
as if others are watching
with me
spying dots of light
through birch leaves, its canopy
speaking one word
down to cool lawn and roses
while another rises up
through mist, steam
of water-light
that turns my house odd, observably other
no longer mine, belonging to another

I imagine *him*
collecting rocks
piled in the blue bowl, some
with origins etched: China, Graz
Venice, Berlin, Lake Winnipeg
—a traveller then, pack laden
granite or sedimentary shale
to hold in any weather
or even taste
He lives among books and plants
Light comes in all windows
and calls him out to sit
near the mallow, ground-cover
gone mad with summer damp

The laurels hold
the moods of this man, they infect me
in his old wooden chair listening
to its lichens tell their story
of change, as we pause
and gaze at the garden
settle on feverfew
reflect on fluid realities
that arrive
with rain

WINTER BROKEN

January with its hammer-sky of grey
its low drop forcing his mind down
into his neck, all brainstem and yet
no primal savvy, that month broke him

so when he arrived at spring what spoke
was not an urge to join chorus-in-song
but only desire to be relieved of
continuing dark-and-thin

How rejoice at Easter's uprising
when all juices had flowed into fits
of fighting constant clouds and rain
and worse: cheerful joggers shouting

to one another how they loved the soft
mist soaking into sweating pores
Not even more light mattered now—
now that heedless plants came up

and punctured his greening lawn
with their charge to him: Spring from haze
and sing the eternal-return tune with us:
what's rot but time made manifest

matter with no beat, turning sweet
then sour, the stink you put away
"His last winter . . ." some speculate
how the madness of spring had never been his

—and still they think he's here in trees
pushing inflorescence forward, and they find
they love him more because he's near, prickly
as wet spruce needles, fast as passing scent

RAISED WITH DOGS

> Most good poets recognize the corked
> wine and fall silent.
>
> —Conor O'Callaghan

Because I was raised with dogs I've seen
their glum look as they enter a certain age
just as I'd watched horses wait long hours
in the shade of poplars, slowly switching
silken tails while nearby snakes split the grass
cats pounce on voles, children cavort
and mystify their parents with their lies

Bright trees wave in wind and then drop
one night all their leaves and thereafter
are silent, revealing themselves as
mere twigs strung together for a nest
where a gawkling crept from a shell
and was pushed, stumbled off its edge
into space, and when spring pressed
his breast open, then he sang and sang

Miles beyond all this unfolding nature
(and unnatural unfolding: boys wicked
with weaner pigs, girls gone slow
around their winking porky uncles)
down the dusty road and into the CNR
station, along wooden boards, up
into steam and iron working a whistle

he's taken to a destination: afternoon irony
coffee clashes, knowledge on display

and later with the solitary wine
tasting cork bits bobbing in the glass
that he tips back, knowing dismay
because he cannot return, reverse
to what he was, that dash of time
among willows, watching wild ducks
float in dignity far from alarming land—
and ahead his dogged look deepening
nothing worth howling about but howling
nonetheless, refusing to whimper
holding back silence with a warning bark

NEXT

Who can say who will return
in the next life as a nymph, willing
to lie down with man after man
one with black hair on his hands
another with thick lips and horn-
rimmed glasses calmly put aside
or a sad, restless humpbacked retiree
skin shiny and slightly damp
and others by evening too indistinct
to recall once they have sucked
stopped shouting and shuddering
and rolled off your firm bed
looked down at your rug as if
defeated before remembering to exalt
to pull on shapeless underpants
to snap suspenders, and wipe
with a white hanky and tuck
and tidy up their new-gained selves

and you talk with the other women
about afternoon soaps you like
an endlessly playing love story
hero's thin malevolent moustache
woman with a far-gone look
how you never see that moment
after their lips meet and they descend
to linen—not that you need compare
what happens up there to
sweating here in these rooms

with their thin walls, their wails
where some cosmic work plays
upon you when each man stumbles
forward following his sex
whatever size and shape and says
save me so I can live without thinking
endlessly, endlessly of putting my
heart-skin near to you, the you
I need now but do not
linger over, leaving behind my
momentary glimmer, my man-time
beyond which you've learned to slide

CELEBRATION

Propped pillow, ice chips, tissues
but none of the apparatus of dying
no blood drained or tubes
no monitors, footfalls, sputum
I am surrounded by all who love me
no one stepped out for a smoke
and each beloved one urging me
to complete myself by going
beyond sense, senseless at last

They do not cry or wring their hands
for they see I have already
become light, they know
I will reach that full brightness
—like snow, only burning—
fierce flickering of the face
glimpsing unbelievable light
—and some crowded near the door
even envious, wishing themselves
forward into imagining
they too will arrive radiant
at an end-night

Yes, everyone is here, all of you
though I failed at first to recognize
one or two who came from
so very far away, jet lines
feathering out from eyes
upper atmosphere
still roaring in your ears

yet none too tired to bring
carried close, the future
kept warm through icy emptiness
angel face so open it's bland
turned away, attuned to a command
beyond my calling him to help
draw out of me one final satisfying yelp

MUSE

She is in the next room
She is not in the next room
She is offshore, on a freighter
  counting fish
She is bringing me tea
  in a white cup
She has no face
She has the face of madness
  and bloody hands
  to prove it
She can do better
whenever she wants to
  but not tonight
She takes me shopping
and lets me feel the cloth
  before taking off
  with a guy's cologne
  touching her lapels
She walks well
stride for stride
easing up on hills
stepping slowly
  when the ground goes down
Keeps waving at me
  from unsuspected places
shouting while I'm driving by
rain muffling
her salute on corners

under the light of a computer company
sign   She goes away

I CANNOT READ ALL THE PURPLE BOOKS

I cannot read all the purple books
yet left, nor can I manage
the green ones, the blue ones
the slim red volumes
that speak an author's innards
as if he's taken a penknife . . .
but I will not give away
the secret endings of the
yellow and yellowing more
old tomes stuck in rows
that make me think here at last
is life, better life than life itself
I lay them upon my chest
as I lie dreaming in the world
they make up, more upset
than mine, for mine is mostly
deciding to leave the couch
for tea, then coming back
through pages haunted and driven
and maddened and shrill
and at times funny but in the main
haunted and driven, mad
Sometimes I have to put them down
face down upon the floor
because the phone is ringing
and I hear ". . . six months . . ."
". . . was good . . ." ". . . no, nothing . . ."
". . . the end . . ."

EARTHWARD

But isn't earth where all of me belongs?
My heart and lungs, my hair, my toes?
    The place exists where all must go:
    the ground, or air. And beyond,
we consider space, which nothing
seems to find, no touch or song, no wing.

My hands will scrabble to the end,
dancing on bed's tight sheet,
    drumming, and speaking, as they repeat
    some coded sign, some message sent
—and when they stop—and so do I—
what goes, what says goodbye

to earth (voice a little sad, I'm sure)?
All I've been I've been by being here.
    No faithfully duplicated me will clear
    his throat and ask: Will then the pure
fly on as well, the might-be-said
when nothing earthward lies ahead?

3.

The Fly in Autumn

THE FLY IN AUTUMN

Yes, the light
        once more
                comes down
                                at last
through clouds
to warm my blue ass
here on the yet green nettle leaf, summer
near the bear plop, and we the species
best at finding dung, in this end light
or in the glow of an early planet

And even so, my wings
carry me, and what thinness
upon which to rely

SINKING

One morning he woke up and started sinking
down through flannel sheets, through foam—
through each airspace in foam—his fingers
clutching what he kept missing, missing it
when he opened his hand, nothing there and
the same nothing kept with him as he sank

down through cloth, coils and then
through his parquet floor, and he panicked
when he entered the ceiling of those
who lived below—but they were workers
and they had already left, their bedsheets
untidy, and he couldn't help noting

pants on the floor, a tube of lipstick tipped
on the dresser, its lid off, the living colour
alarmingly red, and he descended
through shag rug musty with crumbs
and unswept hairs, sock fuzz, toenails
and once a glitzy button passed by

He began to relax now he knew he could
manage ceilings and floors, believing
he would stop when he met hard earth
so down through six discrete floors
he fell, slowly, almost as one drifting, not
plummeting, not a disaster, just a descent

He waved goodbye to operational apparatus
in the basement and then easily entered
concrete and felt the first brisk cold muscle
of buried earth so long removed from light
and incalescence, and knew he would continue
until he met the central fire of the globe

and he wondered if heat at the heart
would be his final immolating destination
if that forge would provide the brake
he needed—but already he was thinking
it hardly mattered where he finally ceased
because the journey toward heat would be

long, long, much longer than six floors
and he would need to settle into accepting
this fate if he wanted any clear mind left
when he came face to face with molten flame
calling him, undoubtedly calling, though last night
he could not have imagined any such sound

GOOFY ME . . .

to imagine a quiet harbour-side
morning coffee, mulling on
how changing light from water's sharpness
allows us to take up purpose
by assigning future hours
(me to home-side gardening
or Ovid or Kurt Wallander)

until that troop of goofy people
arrives—and fuelled by their disruption
such a word rises fast
a circled group
of wheelchairs parked at tables
squeals erupting from odd throats
high pitched, like seagulls
but rustier, some gear
grinding, two women talking
as if alone with one another
their patience extending
impossible for it ever to stop

You have a handicapped cousin?
Then you shouldn't be reading this—
my momentary exasperation presupposes
someone less sensitive, like me
who supposedly still must learn
why fate or spirit or Randomness
allows my hand to hold a coffee with ease
whereas two tables away

a cup is squeezed and dropped
and a body rocks, plaintive keening
setting up a group lowing
—and here my own strangled voice
insists on saying—
like cattle fenced off from water
and a boy coming with his switch
no inkling of animal thirst
so he passes by a wired-up gate
whistling, not loving but
lopsided, not yet tender

INSURANCE

Insurance offices are full of fat men
(cramped behind small desks stacked
    with forms and notes) willing to act
    as agents while chewing on a time when
they were slim with a full head of hair.
This one's thinking of lunch, the éclair,

what the French call *lightning*, and rightly too,
the way it enters the mouth and announces
    the tongue loves custard, not ounces,
    but pounds of soft, long chocolate choux,
an oblong from the oven that combines
fine flour and Jersey cream (I know the kind

he's yearning for). Meanwhile, I sit before him,
and my own youth rises up and smirks,
    a callow, thin judge of this man's work
    we all know will not make him slim;
date-stamping my file and taking my cheque
only ensure little jiggles along his bullish neck.

HEROIC MEASURES

When the dream said my lingo was stale,
used up, degraded down to lists,
    a thin lady with blue wrists,
    her face pinched, and pale
and stinking of a passé perfume,
suddenly materialized in my bedroom.

She leaned, then fell, I felt her grasp
for me, my feet entangled in her clothes,
    her smell going up my nose
    enough to make me gasp.
Worse was her hose hooked up, her blouse
falling open but not enough to rouse

passion in me, oh no, except
I knew here was our chance:
    nothing beats romance
    at halting death. To intercept
her downward arc, I arranged her limbs and hair
just so, breathed into her until she flared.

NIGHT WATCHMAN THINKS . . .

> The dead are happier dead. They don't
> miss much here, poor devils.
> —Harry Lime, in Graham Greene's
> *The Third Man*

. . . if self-destruction is merely
acceleration, give me that Camel
hand me your pearly pills
pass that golden jug
and, while you're at it, Harry's .45
because I want to go faster than death
before death stops for me
I want to lap up life and beyond
before beyond is where I'll . . .

Night watchman on smoke break
steps into gloom corralled by mesh fence
painted green, stiff and leaning
he's breathing white stuff in, wants past
his human minimum potential position
fast fast, home to his woman
and hearth though he has none
but a blue flick-eye in a corner
yet such failure makes him laugh
once he finds his smoke and pills
and, if need be, Harry's
hand-moulded heavyweight sure-fire
entryway into acceleration

because he says the unaccelerated life
is not worth living
drone-flat headache-coming heart-empty time
of too much waiting cannot be borne
without some abrupt jumped-up joy
a little, anyway, let it enter and surge
and please me up, he says, make happiness
happen now, here, fast fast
before dawn must scratch my eyes awake
and make of me/mock me
the still-living long face of misery

SIGHTINGS

I'll have to admit
it's been happening now
for some time, sightings
at the corner
of my eye: mice dashing
so fast I can glimpse
only dark brown
and what feels like fur
—and on bad days

rats, not big
but humpy enough
to unsettle vision
—like that night
on Kootenay Lake
in the dark with friends
I saw stars fall
and then burn up, big
as fridges turned to gas
and dust, leaving behind
a brief beauty
a collective exclamation—

so from my brain
vermin dash out
to cross the room
before I spot them

And when I flinch, they're gone
—no chance to shout
whatever word would work
on such creatures
flashing their mere seconds

THE BLIND NURSE

When your eyes fail
you quit the job of rounds
and reports to the station
and work instead
from front room of your house
a venture, to keep your hand
on others, getting at
what sickens them, through sound
and touch, smell of their
bodies, like lemon sometimes
like rust

You refuse to deal
in splints
or ragged pain
You sit across from me
hold my arm below the elbow
and find where my body is burning
I come for touch of your hands
not so big as I expect
like my mother's

I can watch you without
turning aside, can nurse my hunger
to stare frankly at a face
—what a blessing you give:
that I need not always
be glancing away
I'll leave my money on the corner table

No one ever thinks of cheating you
Sometimes I want to touch your hair
where it is not quite combed

SUCH VAST STILL SPACES

Such vast still spaces exist between us
we cannot know who we might be
and even as we touch an elbow, an arm
we stand alone, shifting our eyes away

We cannot know who we might be
inside our skins and somewhere else besides
when we stand alone, shifting our eyes away
shuffling our feet, eager to run

Inside our skins and somewhere else besides
we try to connect, converse, but
shuffling our feet, eager to run
we might as well be trees, struck down

We try to connect, converse, but
unable to reach across that space
we might as well be trees, stuck down
in the earth, air charged all around

Unable to reach across that space
we leave one another at last
in the earth, air charged all around
by prayers or thoughts or rage

Yes, we leave one another at last
and as we touch an elbow, an arm
with prayers or thoughts or rage
such vast space still exists between us

LEFT HANDCUFF

. . . on July's wrist: a whitish band
across darker sun-kissed skin
pale strap where time holds on
and fine hairs rise and shine
on parchment, blue-pencil lines

leading into knuckle valleys
the exuberance of pink
creased in the palm, a crisscross tale
and fingers' free outstretching
streaming toward another's grip

that pleasant imprisonment of
entwining, then touching key knobs
on the spine, a jazzy song
playing year round and for life
but best in easily unclothed summer

when sunscreen decides to slow
the day, now light has come to stay
and organized parts relax, drink
unmeasured, hands slack
worn sandal dangling from a golden toe

poking another's yet-white softness
on the under arm, so smiles tease loose
curve beneath boaters just now
lifted on salt breezes into water
and becoming the freely blown away

MAKE PEACE WITH INEVITABILITY

and everything else is sweet
—all yawning, ditching, double-dipping
particularity that looked out of me
at the woman walking at the quay
saw her tangled straw hair
pulled back by a ribbon
three strands so tight they aged her

So, yes, assign birth and death, yes
to breathing, living, being river in the head
and other pan-humanic
traits we all have been given to *do*
but then leap beyond into *you*
singing your song all day
happy or sad, understood or not
by others also singing
centres of their own

She brings greasy food, hot, man
getting his fingers in, brackets around his mouth
focused on fish and fries
his red hair sticking up above
liquid mix of his face

I ask: what have they met and matched
and put behind them—
have they bought each other clothes
her floral summer shift floating

in waterfront breeze or his white shirt risking stains
—too young yet for wills?

I wander off to my own death
placidly up ahead, some nexus of age and place
announcing itself too quickly
or a guest lingering too long to bear

still, however, in hibernation
not coming toward me—toward us, the
couple snatching a snack before
his untannable Scottish skin, his thriving summer
takes that pale darling up to some apartment loft
for the fun of stopping time
—and their little deaths kindly find
the harbour's murmuring night
itself happy to be not yet the dawn

SUDDENLY THE RAIN COMES . . .

so horns blare out at mothers
running with children, heads wet
and only patches under trees
still dry with dust where nothing reaches
for a longer time, and where I sit

and imagine what crosses
from wet to dry, from living to
non-living, how an inside gives way and flattens
and takes itself beyond
what I can see:

crows acrobating through
leaves dancing with each ping down
of rain, patio chairs filling up, no one
near although ghosts may come
now and then to drink from their former lives

that little drop hanging on
there by the plastic table
umbrella pointing crookedly up
into what washes and washes me
into the deep of my own cells

past the face and ache
and fall and drip of a moment
whipped inside out and useless
my papers lifted by wind
then weighted by rain

all words slurred, down
with the leaves, joining flashing water
as it bounces and pools
and decides at last to roll
toward some greater settlement
to set out on the journey westward

SORROWFUL FRIENDS

They will always be with us, with their news
of calamity that makes our chests
    feel some old collapse of our own, a protest
    against divergence, a bruise
on last bits of skin we thought still fresh
and fairly managing the task of presenting flesh

to a world aimed at it. Not just sticks and stones,
those wounds heal if not too deep,
    but the injury that makes us weep,
    the one from loving lips, moans
remembered and annulled now by the hard
angle of someone leaving, and someone scarred.

What can I say to my friends?[†] Nothing much
that will give them solace. "I too have suffered"
    hardly counts as any useful buffer
    against the loss of *we* and loss of touch.
Before long, I'll meet each on the street, one here
and another there, on separate days, in a different year.

---

†

Practise speaking what needs to be said.
Let the old words go, let them fall away
    like last year's leaves, their last day
    forgotten: let them be dead.
You need a new tongue now
to savour once and then disavow

forever those love poems mouthed at night,
the joy of saying wet nouns,
    verbs that sounded
    true, the delight
you assumed was ever-meant,
hands on one another, purely spent.

Find your former selves in dreams
where passion-paired once more
    you share the pouring
    thoughts that need no streams
of words to work—But for now you must
change your life, give up speaking dust.

SOMEONE I KNOW

Someone I know is dying
living the days one by one by one
while the body plans its flight
beyond the wide, tiled hallway
and someone else I know—and love—
has fallen in love, has found the one
who makes her want to be herself
on earth all day long

and still crows hurry at dusk
to roosts where young hatch out
to squawk at mothers' bills
until they fly and forget
they are bonded to the ground
by trees, though above us

How we manage
the dying and the loving
our hearts big steamy
sites believers come to
point at, photograph
because here they say a human
did his work each morning
though dying was coming too

Did he walk along the shore and think
the hundred thousand thoughts
everyone collects in a day?
Did he find a separate self

tugged by those loved and leaving?
Does he see, still, the stones
he flung into waves
sinking below their circles?

HOUSEHOLD

Everywhere at hand
the implements and habits
of familiar ease

where hip breaks against door
the flu comes knocking
a fever of flame

the trash piles up
around where clothes
wait to trip

I could of course crash
my car or be crushed
on the sidewalk by some
mad drunk
                    but out there
the comfort of a pile of leaves
the water's lip
the sky one day I'll excarnate
into

until I am plunged back
to see beyond shoulders
of two who peer down
in welcome and worry
at my new toes

and I spot the bother
of what I'll learn to call
utensils, cats, fires
the long hallway
leading to
                    air

POEM AGAINST THE RETURNING ANGEL

From my shoulders down to my hips
what am I?—the day I was made
every cell borrowed
from parents what they got
from God—and each cluster
will be recalled
when the bestower returns, sent across time
for gut, glands or lungs
—Heart will not protest much
when it feels him fingering
and my liver will shine
with unearthly light once
plopped in unstainable bowls—

but my arms can fend off
his advent—I can run
and kick, strike at him
who comes to collect mid-section
freight previously signed for
—watch me hurl stones
upward into his descending, soundless
plumes—let him underestimate
nails of my hands
bones of my fingers—
right heel can break an
intended embrace—
I can determine to fight

or love: look up
close the eye
unsure mouth and, last of all
seashell curves of the ear

THE NEW PIER

attracts so few of us, its concrete walkway
with identical ladders descending into water
(how far? from here no one can tell)
and behind its open space
grand dry docks held to the sky
by long pulleys and large spotlights
not leisure

of the sort found here, where we see
an escaped balloon run away
and tugs rear back and circle off
in rubber-nosed purpose, every man leaning
out beyond bright red rails
watching, women less gripped

Over there, a solitary walker
glides under windsocks that hang inert
and though he ventures beyond our endpoint
closer to ships, closer to the centre deep
does he see anything more

than a black cormorant on guard
skimming the top inch of waves, one white gull
floating in air different from his own
a tight flock of seven pigeons
oblivious to beauty and heading downtown?